Women
of the Bible

Margaret McAllister

ILLUSTRATED BY
Alida Massari

PARACLETE PRESS
BREWSTER, MASSACHUSETTS

For *Matilda Grace*   M.M.
To my little *Diana*   A.M.

2013 First Printing this Edition

Women of the Bible

Text copyright © 2013 Margaret McAllister

Illustrations copyright © 2013 Alida Massari

Published in the United States and Canada by Paraclete Press, 2013.

ISBN: 978-1-61261-372-7

Original edition published in English under the title *Women of the Bible* by Lion Hudson plc, Oxford, England.
Copyright © 2013 Lion Hudson plc

The right of Margaret McAllister to be identified as the author and of Alida Massari to be identified as the illustrator of this work has been asserted by them in accordance with the Copyright, Designs and Patents Act 1988.

10 9 8 7 6 5 4 3 2 1

Published by Paraclete Press

Brewster, Massachusetts

www.paracletepress.com

Printed and bound in China.

Contents

Mother Noah

R ESCUING ANIMALS IS only the start of it," said Mother Noah. She scooped up a handful of seeds and placed them carefully in her pocket. "If God wants to send a flood, it's very good of him to ask Noah to put the animals in a boat. But *then* what do you do with them?"

Then, having said her bit, she put on her waterproof coat and boots and took her place on the deck of the ark. Far below, she could see Mr Noah and their sons, Ham, Shem, and Japheth, at the bottom of the gangplank, but she couldn't look down for long. The height made her dizzy. This boat was enormous. To Mother Noah, it looked like a huge toy box for huge toy animals (with one very important difference).

Above her, the rain clouds were gathering. Below, so were the real animals. Here they all came, hurrying and scurrying, bounding and bouncing, loping and lumbering, padding and plodding, pacing, racing, from every direction, more and more of them, and some of them with such teeth and claws that Mother Noah just hoped they weren't hungry. She moved over to the top of the gangplank with her sons' wives, Hannah, Susie, and Jo, ready to take the animals to their cabins, "Always hoping," she thought, "that we don't get trampled to death in the first rush."

Mr Noah raised a hand. Mother Noah looked down at two approaching lions, offered up a prayer to God, and grabbed a stout stick.

"Courage," she told herself. "I've brought up three boys. A few hundred animals can't be much worse. Can they?"

The lions weren't a problem. They were well fed and only wanted to sprawl on the top deck. (They were meant to be in the hold, but Mother Noah decided not to argue with them.) The elephants and tigers were quiet, too. The family had more trouble with the small cats (catching them), the mice (finding them before the cats did), the caterpillars (finding them at all), and the chimpanzees (who liked chasing each other over the roof). By this time the rain was falling steadily, which at least meant that the cats stopped stalking the parrots and took shelter below decks.

Most of the animals could be put into the right stalls or boxes by coaxing them in with bits of food, apart from the nocturnal ones – badgers, hedgehogs, owls, bushbabies, and anything with big eyes. They were all asleep. When everything else was settling down for the night, they were wide awake and ready to play, and as Susie remarked, the owls wanted to play with the mice.

"We must always keep the mice shut in their cage," said Mother Noah. "It'll be a miracle if they survive this trip."

The four couples took turns with the various duties – feeding, exercising, cleaning out (that was the worst one), and nursing any animals who had toothache, or seasickness, or depression. The bears were soon so fed up that they pretended it was winter and hibernated, which made things easier.

Afterwards, when people asked what life had been like on the ark, Mother Noah said, "Wet." Then she would add, "Boring." It was an endless round of the same dull duties. However much they cleaned, they

never got rid of the smell, and it wouldn't have been so bad if it hadn't been for the forty days of RAIN. (Mr Noah said afterwards it was forty days, but Mother Noah soon gave up counting.) It seemed as if there had never been a time when they hadn't lived on this boat, with wet fur, wet clothes, wet whiskers, wet washing, wet wombats, wet wallabies. The work left Mother Noah tired, aching, and scratched. At the end of every day, she would think, "That's one more day done, and one fewer to do."

But however hard it was, every day brought something good. On day ten the tigers realized that she was a friend and stopped trying to eat her. On day eleven the parrots learned to say, "Move over!" which saved Mother Noah a lot of shouting. On day fifteen the chimpanzees had a very silly half hour with Ham's hat and Mr Noah's whistle. On day thirty an orang-utan fell asleep in her arms. And on day forty-one – the sun came out!

Finally the ark came to rest. The waters ebbed away and the earth grew firm. Steam rose from the decks as they dried in the sun. The animals sniffed nervously as they walked down the gangplank – then, suddenly, under the bright arch of the rainbow, they remembered how they were meant to be, and ran in all directions. They climbed trees, dug holes, chased, built nests, wallowed in mud, and rolled over each other for fun.

"How sad to see them go," thought Mother Noah, with tears in her eyes. "And how lovely to see them go." Then, as the lambs scampered, the monkeys chattered, and the tigers raced away, the people (and some of the animals) hugged each other. Hannah, Susie, and Jo danced and danced for joy.

Mother Noah put her hand into her pocket.

"Time to sow my garden," she said.

Rachel

I<small>T'S NIGHT</small>. It's dark. In Rachel's tent, small flames float on the oil lamps. Men stand outside to guard her and her little boy, Joseph. Rachel's husband, Jacob, is a wealthy man with more flocks and herds than anyone in these lands, but his greatest treasure is in this tent: Rachel, his favourite wife, and Joseph, their son.

Today all of Jacob's people – his wives, sons, the people who work for him, and their immense herds of animals – crossed the River Jabbok. Tomorrow they will meet Jacob's brother, Esau. Tonight, where is Jacob?

All night he will stay on the other side of the river. Not even Rachel knows why. She is anxious for him and can't sleep.

Joseph, snug as a dormouse in his nest of fleeces, sleeps peacefully. His long, dark eyelashes brush his tanned cheek, and Rachel looks down at him with love so strong she can hardly bear it. She waited a long time to have this child.

She wraps a sheepskin around herself and thinks of their story. It's twenty years since she and Jacob first met, by the well where she was giving water to her father's sheep. Jacob was running away from trouble at home and trying to find his Uncle Laban, hoping to work for him. He'd asked if she knew Laban and she'd laughed. Laban was her father! So she and Jacob were cousins and,

what's more, they were in love from that moment.

Jacob had gone to work for Laban, and the only payment he had asked for was to marry Rachel. Laban had agreed, but only if Jacob worked for him for seven years first. Seven years was a long time, but they were engaged and happy.

Rachel frowns. It wasn't that simple. She had an elder sister, Leah, and the two of them never got on well. Rachel saw Leah getting everything first – Leah was the first to wear grown-up clothes and stay up late with the adults. Leah thought Rachel was the spoilt baby and, besides, Rachel was the pretty one.

In Laban's country, the elder sister must always be married before the younger one, but as the seven years went by, there weren't any plans to find a husband for Leah. If Rachel asked her father about it, he just smiled and said nothing.

In the darkness, Rachel sits forward and hugs her knees. She doesn't like to think of the next part of her story. She would rather forget the day that should have been her wedding day.

All the women were finely dressed, with beautifully embroidered veils over their faces so that only their eyes showed. Leah's eyes, she thinks bitterly, were the most beautiful thing about her. It was easy for Laban to trick Jacob.

Rachel still sheds a few tears when she thinks about it. Laban had forced her to keep silent and she could only stand and watch as Jacob, completely fooled, had made his marriage promises to Leah. It was only the next morning when he'd realized what had happened.

Rachel curls her hands and clenches her teeth as she remembers Jacob's rage, her own fury, and the smug expressions on the faces of Laban and Leah. At the end of the week, Jacob had been married to her, too, but he had had to work another seven years for the privilege.

She walks to the opening of the tent and looks up. She has never seen so many stars, seeming so low and so close that she could reach up and touch them. She thinks of them shining on Jacob in the darkness on the other side of the river.

Her thoughts run quickly through the next years of her life: the long years when she was childless. Leah was first, as usual, giving birth to Jacob's first son.

And the second, the third, and the fourth. Every time Leah appeared, beaming with joy, carrying another healthy baby boy, Rachel had to look away. She had been so desperate that she had followed an old custom and given her servant girl, Bilhah, to Jacob. Bilhah's babies would be counted as if they were Rachel's. So then Leah, mother-of-four Leah, still wanted to impress Jacob and gave him her servant girl, too. Even those two servants gave Jacob sons! Pain and jealousy had torn Rachel's heart in those times, and she had almost lost hope. Then, wonderfully, she had felt the first fluttering movements of her own baby.

When they placed tiny, newborn Joseph in her arms, she had wept for love of him. Her own beautiful son. Jacob had wept, too, to have a son by his dearest wife. After that she didn't mind how many big strong boys Leah had. She was sure of Jacob's love, and Joseph was the bright star in their sky.

The thought of Joseph draws Rachel to him and she goes back into the tent to watch him in his sleep. He has inherited his father's intelligence and her own fighting spirit and good looks. He loves to be helpful, fetching and carrying, feeding the animals. He works harder than his older brothers. She wonders what he's dreaming about.

A few weeks ago, the time had come when they had to get away from Laban, who would have kept Jacob working for him for ever, if he could. They had taken their hundreds and hundreds of animals – sheep, donkeys, cattle, goats, even camels

– and come here, to send gifts to Jacob's brother Esau and to try to make peace.

Could they make peace? Twenty years ago, Jacob had tricked Esau and received the Great Blessing from their father Isaac. Good things come to the one who has the Great Blessing and it was meant for Esau, because he was the elder son, though only by a few minutes. Jacob says that Esau didn't care about the Great Blessing; he'd rather have had a day's hunting and a hot dinner. But all the same, Jacob had tricked him out of it, and now, after twenty years, he has come to ask Esau to forgive him. He's sending some of the livestock as a gift for his brother.

The men who went ahead said that Esau was coming with four hundred men. Why does he need four hundred men to greet his brother? Do they come with bows and arrows and swords? The thought troubles Rachel and once more she leaves the tent and looks into the dark for any sign of danger.

Will the morning never come? When will Jacob come back? Rachel prays to God, Jacob's God, the God who sees them, the God who has guided them. She imagines Jacob, too, on the other side of the river, standing in the presence of God and crying out for his blessing.

Now the dawn is coming and, in the half light, she sees a man wading across the river. It is Jacob's shape, but not his walk, because this man is limping. But it *is* Jacob and she wades in to meet him and walk back to the camp with him.

He will not tell her why he's limping, not yet. He does tell her about his plans for this day.

"I'm sending the gifts to Esau first," he says, "then the family, but you and Joseph are last. I think it'll be all right – but if he hasn't forgiven me, if he attacks, turn and run."

So for a long time, as the bleating, lowing, braying creatures are herded onward, Joseph stands by Rachel's side, trying not to fidget, asking her why they have to be last. She tells him it's because we always leave the best until last. She never lets him out of her sight.

The procession moves on. First the servant girls and their children are presented to Esau, then Leah and her children, and at last Rachel steps forward,

holding Joseph by the hand. Jacob and Esau stand side by side, each with an arm around the other, and for the first time she sees Esau, a big man with rough, hairy arms and tears on his red face. She kneels, whispers to Joseph to bow, and rises, giving Joseph's hand a little squeeze. There are tears in her own eyes, too.

"That's how it should be with brothers," she tells Joseph. "Sisters, too, whatever quarrels they have, they must forgive and forget. It's the only way."

Miriam

WHEN MY LITTLE brother Moses was born, my mother cried.

My baby brother didn't do much crying, though. He wasn't allowed to. As soon as he squeaked, he'd be picked up and soothed. Before he could make a sound, he'd be fed, and his dirty cloths changed, and then he'd be rocked to sleep. Nobody must hear him cry.

Those were the terrible years when we were slaves in Egypt. I was a child, but I'll never forget the hot red earth, the long hours in the baking sun, and the brick-making. The sour smell of stale sweat hung in the dry, dusty air. The parents were always too tired to play with us children, and we had to work, too, as soon as we were old enough to fetch and carry. Children who were doing what all children do – chasing each other, hiding, and jumping over ropes – were taken from their games and sent to work until they were too tired to play.

But the slavery wasn't the worst thing. The worst thing was the rule for newborn boys. The Egyptians feared that we Hebrews would soon outnumber them, so their king – the pharaoh – made the most terrible law of all. To this day, it still shocks me when I think of it. Every newborn Hebrew boy was to be killed. Only the girls could live. And that's why my mother cried when she gave birth to a son. And that's why my brother had to be kept quiet and hidden, like so many Hebrew sons. I didn't mind being the one who rocked him, sang to him, even changed him. He was my baby brother and I adored him.

But the time came when my parents knew they couldn't keep him hidden any longer. You can't keep a baby quiet for ever, and soon he'd be crawling, then wobbling about on his feet. What could we do? Every day he grew more beautiful and more precious. He smiled and laughed – a throaty little chuckle that made his whole face light up. He'd hold my finger and try to put it in his mouth. The thought of anyone harming him was unbearable.

One morning I heard my mother saying a prayer. I couldn't hear all she said, but she began praying to our God, the God of Israel, and saying what she always said – "God of Abraham, Isaac, and Jacob" – and then she prayed for my brother.

I prayed, too. Abraham, Isaac, and Jacob were the ancestors, the great men of our Hebrew family. But it was women who brought babies into the world and looked after them.

I thought of the great women of our family and I prayed, "Great God, our God, God of Sarah, Rebecca, and Rachel, look after our baby. Look after our little baby boy and keep him safe."

When my mother had said her prayers, she called me. We went down to the riverside where the rushes grew thick and strong, and came home with our arms full of rushes and long supple reeds. Together we wove a basket with a hood over the top and sealed it with tar to make it waterproof. Then we waited for it to dry, and as we waited, we prayed again: "God of Abraham, Isaac, and Jacob, God

of Sarah, Rebecca, and Rachel, please keep our little boy safe. Send someone to find him, care for him, and protect him. Send somebody who will simply love him and not care about Hebrew or Egyptian, girl or boy, slave or free."

We lined the basket to make it warm and soft, and before dawn my mother took our little boy and laid him in it, tucking him in and settling him down to sleep. I put a muslin cloth over the hood, so no flies could land on his face and bite him, no river frog jump in and frighten him.

Not speaking, because we were close to tears, we carried him down to a place near the river where the basket would be half hidden by the long grasses – but not too well hidden. We wanted someone to find him. Then my mother turned and walked firmly away, but not before I saw the tears roll down her face.

I stayed. I wanted to know what would happen. But I was only a child and I had been up late at night and early in the morning, so I was falling asleep when the sound of voices startled me.

Three young women were coming down to the water, carrying towels, oils, and brushes: all the things that rich people take with them for river bathing. One of them wore gold bracelets and didn't have to carry anything, so I knew she was important.

"This is the best place, Princess," said one of the girls.

Princess! She didn't have to be that important! This was the pharaoh's own daughter! Her father had commanded the killing of the Hebrew babies! My legs felt wobbly with fear. *Oh, please, not her, please God. She'll take him back to the pharaoh's palace and have him killed. Please, God, no.*

There was nothing I could do. My brother lay asleep in his basket in the rushes, and I couldn't stop her from finding him. It was too late. I could hear my own heart beating like the sound of running footsteps. Running away? Or running to help?

"Girls!" said the princess. "There's something in the reeds. Go and see what it is."

As I watched, the princess's maids lifted the cradle and held it high, with grasses and damp weeds clinging to the side, and as they carried it to the

princess, I heard the first faint, sad mews of a cry. Tears came into my eyes and the longing to hold him tore into my heart.

The maids took the muslin from the basket, and the pharaoh's daughter, with her braceleted arms, reached in and lifted out my crying baby brother. His eyes were tightly shut and his voice loud and distressed, and I saw the look that came over the princess's face as she cradled him. It was that "aah" face, the way girls look when they see a baby.

"He's one of the Hebrew baby boys," she said.

Now that he'd been picked up, my brother stopped crying. The princess looked down into his face and put her finger into his hand, and then she didn't see a Hebrew baby at all. She just saw a baby who needed love.

"Never mind, little one," she said in that shushing, pouting way people have with babies. "I'll look after you."

Then I knew exactly what to do and I had to do it *now*. No dithering, no doubting. It was almost like playing a game of chasing, or hiding, or jumping over a rope. You have to dodge, or jump, just at the right moment, or not at all. I dried my eyes, stepped forward, and curtsied to the princess.

"Madam," I said, "would you like a nurse to help you look after the baby? I know a Hebrew woman who would be very good."

"Thank you!" said the princess. "What a good thing you were there! Bring the woman to me immediately."

I ran all the way home to get my mother.

The princess named our baby "Moses". Sometimes I wondered if she guessed who his real mother was.

When Moses grew up, he fought for the rights of the Hebrew people to be free and go to a land of their own. That meant that he had to stand up to the pharaoh time and again, and there was a long, fierce struggle between them before Moses won and led our people to freedom. But I think he won his first battle against the pharaoh when he was three months old, when all the pharaoh's laws and all his power couldn't stop his daughter from loving a baby.

So that's how it was. Three caring women, one helpless crying child, and our God with us. All the might of Egypt couldn't do a thing about that.

Ruth

THERE WAS A story my granny used to tell me, and she always told it the same way.

Long ago, in the land of Moab, there were two best friends called Orpah and Ruth. They went everywhere and did everything together. Then a couple from another country moved in, Elimelech and Naomi. They had two handsome sons called Mahlon and Chilion. Ruth and Orpah fell in love with the brothers and even got married on the same day.

It should have been happy ever after, but it wasn't. Within ten years all the men in that family – Elimelech, Mahlon, and Chilion – had died. Naomi, Orpah and Ruth were left heartbroken, three widows without children. Naomi decided to go back to the place she came from, which was Bethlehem, so Orpah and Ruth both packed their bags to go with her.

"Don't come with me, girls!" cried Naomi. "You've always been good to me, but what sort of a life will you have with me? I can't do anything to help you. Go back to your mothers. Marry again; be happy."

Finally Orpah did as Naomi said and went home, crying. But Ruth hugged Naomi and said, "I won't leave you, Naomi. You're my family, and I'm yours. You've lost your husband and your sons, so how can I leave you now? I will live in your country and worship your God."

Well, they got home to Bethlehem just as the barley in the fields was ripe and the farmers were harvesting the crop. Now, whenever the reapers went out, cutting the crops and gathering them up, they never cut right to the edge of the field. If they dropped a few bits, they didn't go back for them. They always left some for poor people to gather up and take home, so they wouldn't go hungry. Gathering up the leftover grain was called "gleaning".

Naomi and Ruth moved in to a little house in Bethlehem with whatever they brought with them, which wasn't much. So, first thing in the morning, Ruth took a bag and went straight out to the fields to glean. Like all the other gleaners, she kept her head bent and her eyes to the ground, watching. It was a sunny day. Her back ached and she grew hot and thirsty, but she kept working.

A shadow fell across her, keeping the hot sun from her back. She looked up. There, looking down at her, was a tall man, dressed as a farmer, but she thought that those were very nice sandals for a farmer, and his hair was well cut.

"Oh, help!" thought Ruth. "He's the owner of this field and he's going to send me away!"

But the man smiled down kindly. "You're Ruth, aren't you?" he said. "My name's Boaz and I've heard how kind you've been to Naomi. Glean in my fields as much as you like. Stay close to the women

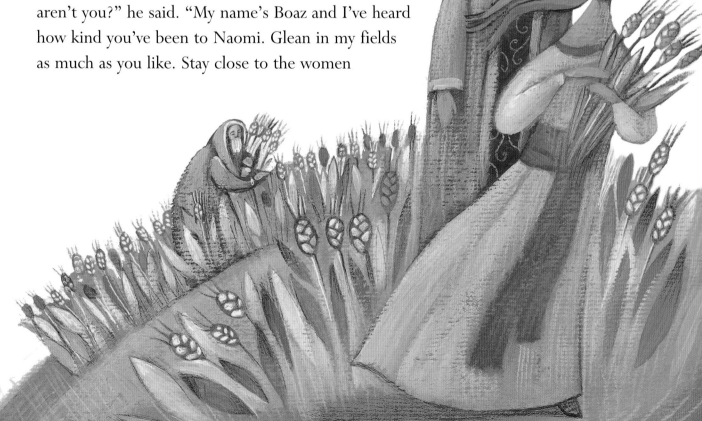

who work for me; they'll look after you. You see those water jars? Take a drink from those whenever you want one."

Ruth hadn't expected such kindness. When Boaz sat down to eat with his workers, he invited Ruth to join them and shared the food with her; there was so much that she had something to take home to Naomi.

The gleaning went amazingly well that afternoon. Boaz's men seemed to be leaving a lot of barley for her. They dropped lots, and didn't go back for it. After a long day's work, she had so much barley that she could barely carry it home to Naomi.

"Where did all that come from?" asked Naomi in astonishment.

"Boaz's field," said Ruth, a bit out of breath as she dropped the bag on the floor. "He was very kind."

"Boaz!" repeated Naomi. "I'm related to him! I'm glad he's looking after you. You've done so well in his fields today that you should go back tomorrow."

By the time the harvest was finished, Boaz and Ruth were in love. To Naomi's delight, they got married and had a beautiful baby boy, and the minute that baby was born, Ruth gave him to Naomi for a cuddle. And Naomi was the happiest woman in the world.

She would tell that story and I would say, "And that was me!"

"Yes, Obed, that was you," she would say.

I'd bounce on the bed and say, "And Ruth and Boaz are Mother and Father, and Naomi is you!"

"And it's bedtime," Granny Naomi would say, and then she'd tuck me into bed and say a blessing over me.

Mary of Nazareth

I<small>F I COULD WRITE</small>, I would remember each day and write it down. Every evening, at the lighting of the lamps and prayer time, I would think over the day and put its story on paper, so I could go back and always remember it as clear and true as when it first happened. But as I can't write, I tell my stories to myself, over and over; and I tell them to Joseph and Jesus, always the same way, as if they are words on a parchment instead of in my head. For the stories of the great moments, the turning points in life, I pick up something to mark them and keep these things in a special box. In my box I keep a feather, a stone, apple pips, and a tuft of sheep's wool. The other things – the three jars – are in a basket on a high shelf.

The Feather Story

We all have moments that come upon us unexpectedly and change our lives for ever. For me, it was the Angel Moment.

The day was full of weaving, collecting water, chatting, and scrubbing vegetables, until something happened – I don't know exactly what – but it was like finding myself in one of the old stories from the Scriptures. The archangel Gabriel was there, in my world, making everything buzz with joy and hope. He told me of the baby I was to have – the one-and-only, God-with-us baby, Jesus: the Son of God. Then, just as suddenly, he wasn't there, and I had nothing but the memory of him and his message.

I looked up and saw only a dove flying over the house. A feather floated down and landed at my feet. I kept that feather.

The Stone Story

We started out before dawn, because it was such a long way to Bethlehem, where we had to go for the census. I had never journeyed so far in my life, and it wasn't a good day for travel. I was so full of baby that I couldn't get comfortable. I walked at first, but it wasn't long before Joseph took the bedding rolls off the donkey and put me on there instead. Poor donkey!

Finally we got a lift on a cart and jiggled over the stony road while I sat with my hand on my bump, telling my baby it would be all right. To be honest,

I thought the angel would have taken more care of us than this. My back hurt so much that sometimes I had to grit my teeth.

I felt a bit better when we all stopped at a well to draw water and let the donkey drink. I picked up a stone – a round, flat one, with a rough brown top that looked like a round bread cake – to remind me of our journey and the dreadful roads. We ended up in a stable, of all things! Oh, well. It was good of the landlady to clear a space in it for us – she was so busy. "It's just for the census," I thought to myself. "Then we can go home."

The Apple Story

I thought it was just the long, rough journey that made me ache so much, but as the pain become strong and regular, I knew that this was it. My baby was coming. He wasn't going to wait until I was home and safe in my own bed, with my mother not far away.

I bit on my fist so I wouldn't cry. It wasn't just the pain; it was the fear, not knowing how much worse it would get, or what to do. I even began to wonder if I had really seen an angel that day in spring, and where he was now, when I needed him. I must have screamed, because the landlady came and stood at the doorway with her hands on her hips, telling us to stop all that noise – but when she saw I was in labour, she changed completely. She brought water and clean rags and even a cloth to wrap the baby in.

Five minutes later Jesus was in my arms – my baby, my son, with his tiny hands curled up and his eyes blinking in the lamplight – and I forgot all the pain. The landlady cleaned out the hay from the feeding manger and made a makeshift cot for Jesus, and then she brought me a warm drink and an apple, saying I must eat and keep up my strength. She'd sliced the apple across, and the pattern of the seed pods and pips made a star.

As I turned to tell Joseph about the star, light was shining through gaps in the stable roof, light that sparkled like sunlight on silver. I was looking at another star, a real one this time, bright and low in the sky, brighter than any star I've ever seen.

"There's a star," I said to Joseph. He went out to look, and as he opened the door, music billowed into the stable! I'd never heard such lovely music, but I knew what it was and it lifted my heart. The angels were singing for their king. They hadn't left me.

I took out the apple pips and kept them to take home. I'm going to plant a tree that will grow with Jesus.

The Fleece Story

We were still wide awake, watching the star and listening to the music, when the shepherds arrived. They looked dazzled, talking about angels singing and sending them here, but they hadn't forgotten their manners. They stood in the doorway, wiping their sandals before they came in, and bowed their heads as they knelt before Jesus. I always thought shepherds were rough, but these were honest, kind men, gentle and sincere. They didn't stay long – they said they didn't want to tire me and, besides, they had their sheep to look after – and they left us a present of warm, soft fleeces.

With the snuggly warm fleeces and the soft music, I drifted into sleep for an hour or two, then woke feeling the fleece against my cheek. I can spin this wool. It'll make winter clothes for Jesus when he's a bit bigger.

The Three Jars

Late one night, when I'd fed Jesus and settled him down and we were all packed up, ready to leave Bethlehem in the morning, there was such a commotion outside! Horses' hooves, a clattering of harness, voices – Joseph opened the door to see what was the matter only to be greeted by three very excited men, beaming with delight, bowing low and asking to see the new king! They pointed up to the star and said it had led them to us!

We welcomed them in and they dropped to their knees in front of Jesus. They came from lands I'd never heard of and wore the strangest robes, decorated with patterns of vine leaves and fishes, but they were old robes that had seen better days. I got the impression that these men knew there were more important things than clothes. They didn't seem bothered about the fact that we were poor and just about everything we had for the baby was borrowed. Then they brought out the gifts in the three jars.

One was gold. Gold! I hardly dared accept it, but I would have offended them if I hadn't. It was their way of proclaiming Jesus as a king. The second was incense, as a sign of worship and prayer. Then there was myrrh, and I flinched. Myrrh! It's for embalming the dead – the old – and how could they give that to my beautiful newborn baby?

And then I understood that one day my son would die, as other men die, and that there is no life without pain. Any woman who's just had a baby knows that. Will I ever fully understand my son? Perhaps one day he will go where I don't want him to go and say things that trouble me, and even leave behind the protection of the angels.

But not yet, my darling boy. Not yet.

Martha and Mary

MARTHA AND MARY. Big sister Martha was the bossy one – she never stood still. She was always busy and expected everybody else to be the same. Little sister Mary was the quiet, thoughtful one – never hurried, seemed to live in a world of her own. We all wondered how they could bear to live together in the same house.

They argued, as sisters do. They argued the day Jesus came to visit them, and after he'd gone, they were still at it. With the door open, you could hear Martha three doors down.

"Thank you very much, Mary! It's all very well now, you standing there, washing up! All the time Jesus was here, all the time we had a house full of people, you just sat there at his feet like a cabbage!"

"I don't know what you mean," said Mary calmly. She could be exasperating like that. "I was listening to Jesus. That's why he was here. He did explain that to you."

"Don't pretend it was his idea that you sat and did nothing. I wasn't asking much, was I? Just to get everyone a drink, to serve the soup while it was hot…"

"But they didn't come for drinks and soup – they came to listen to Jesus."

"I'm not talking about *them*!" Martha snapped back. "I'm talking about *you*!

You're family – you should have looked after our guests!"

"But they didn't want to be looked after!" insisted Mary. "All they wanted was to sit and hear what Jesus had to say. They wanted to learn."

"But it wasn't *your* place to sit there, learning!" stormed Martha. "It was your place to serve up, and where were you? Sitting there, in the best place in the room, and gazing up at him so I couldn't even catch your eye!"

"Jesus didn't mind."

"I know Jesus didn't mind, but I DID!" yelled Martha and, do you know, there was a touch of tightness in her voice as if she might cry. "You can be so selfish! Didn't it occur to you that I might have wanted to listen, too?"

"Then you should have done," said Mary simply. "That was what he meant when he told you that you were trying to do lots of things, and only one thing was necessary. He was inviting you to sit down, too."

"And the soup would have served itself, I suppose." Martha sounded very close to tears. "Soup and bread is what I'm good at and he scorned it, in front of everyone!"

"He didn't scorn it!" said Mary. "He just thinks you're more important than soup."

Martha didn't often cry, but now she did, sobbing like a child. It was a while before she could control her voice.

"I wanted to listen," she said at last. "I wanted to hear what he said – that's why I invited him. But there were all those people, and I wanted to do things properly. And I kept looking at you, to get you to come and help, and you didn't even glance at me – and it was all going to be so wonderful, and it all went wrong. And I missed hearing his stories!"

"Oh, Martha," said Mary gently, "I'm sorry. I didn't realize you felt like that. But I heard every word, so I can tell you everything he said. I can tell you his stories."

There was a loud sniff from Martha and then she said, "Do you think he'll ever come back?"

"I should think so," said Mary. "It was such nice soup! Listen, if he comes back, you just sit and listen and don't worry about food, or the washing up, or bowls of things to nibble at. Just listen to him. Leave the kitchen to me."

Martha and Mary. Sisters. How could they live in the same house?

How could they not?

The Canaanite Woman

M<small>Y LITTLE GIRL</small> had an answer for everything.

I'd say, "Time for bed, Eppy."

"But I'm not tired," Eppy would say.

"You will be, by the time you've had your bath and your story."

"I might not be."

"I think you will. Bed, Eppy."

"But it's still daylight."

"That's because it's summer. Bed now, or there won't be time for a story."

"Oh, Mother! Not fair!"

She had a lot of questions, too. Most of them began "Why?" or "Why not?" and I didn't always have answers.

Her grandmother got so cross! She'd tell Eppy to do as she was told and not answer back. If Eppy asked, "Why is the sky blue?" she'd say, "Because it is!" But I loved it – I loved the way Eppy asked and thought and worked things out.

The day she fell ill it just looked as if she'd been in the sun too long. I brought her indoors, into the shade, and sponged her down. But she didn't cool down. Her skin was burning to touch and as dry as brushwood. We bathed her and gave her cooling drinks that she didn't want to take, but nothing worked.

My husband, coming back from his work at the harbour, said that there was a famous Jewish rabbi staying at the white house near the sea.

"What's a Jewish rabbi doing anywhere around Sidon?" said mother.

"Trying to get some peace and quiet," he said, "but I wonder if he could help our Eppy? He's supposed to be a healer. A miracle man, that kind of healer. His name's Jesus of Nazareth, and he healed a woman in…"

"He's Jewish and we're not," interrupted my mother. "He's not going to help us, is he? Why would he?"

Eppy was ill, so I had to do the arguing for her. *Why wouldn't he?* I ran from the house.

"He won't help us!" my mother called after me. "His God isn't our god!"

"I don't want a god," I thought. "I want Eppy. Run, run, run, keep running."

I ran all the way to the white house, and I must have been shouting out for help as I came nearer, because somebody opened the door. My legs wouldn't hold me up any more and I stumbled to the ground at the rabbi's feet.

"Please, sir," I gasped out, "my little girl – Eppy – she's dying. Please will you come and help her?"

He looked at me, saying nothing at all. The crowd drew back to give him space. Because I was on my knees, he knelt, too, to talk to me, but in his eyes I didn't see what I wanted. I wanted to see somebody who knew the right thing to do and would do it. But he just looked sad.

"Daughter," he said, "I can't help you. God sent me to help my own people, and they need so much from me. I can't go to everyone else too. It would be like taking the children's bread and throwing it to the dogs."

The dogs? Do you think I was angry? Or insulted? Or hurt? I didn't have time to be. Eppy was all that mattered, and she would have had an answer for him. *What would Eppy say?* I thought of Eppy's kind of answer.

"But if you had a dog, and the children dropped crumbs under the table," I said, "you'd let the dogs eat the crumbs, wouldn't you? So what about giving us the crumbs?"

I watched his face. His eyes crinkled at the corners as he smiled.

"You have real faith!" he said. "Go home! Your child is well!"

I hope I remembered to say thank you. I ran home to find Eppy as bright as a button, out of bed, and drinking pomegranate juice.

Years later, Eppy came home and told me she'd joined a group of Jesus' followers – or "Followers of the Way", as they called themselves.

"The way to where?" I asked her and she laughed.

"Come with us," she said, "and you'll find out."

Lady Procula,
the Wife of Pilate

THE SCREAM RAN through the governor's residence, a scream of such
desperation that it hit like a punch in the stomach. Maids scrambled
from their beds, stumbling in the half light, for the sun had not risen. Guards
ran through corridors with drawn swords in their hands, but by the time they
reached Lady Procula's room, Julia was already comforting her ladyship.

Pilate, the Roman governor in Jerusalem, was not at home that night, so
Lady Procula had been sleeping alone in the grand, canopied bed. Her maid,
Julia, had been asleep on a mat on the floor and was now wrapping a shawl
around the lady's shaking shoulders.

Lady Procula sat up as straight as a lance, her face grey with shock, her black
hair tangled over her shoulders, and her dark eyes wide and wild. Julia held her
tightly and waved the guards away.

"My lady has had a nightmare," she told them. "Leave her. Quietly. Is there
anyone here from the kitchen? Go and get a warm drink with lemon balm and
valerian." She reached into a drawer. "Here, madam, I'll put lavender under
your pillow."

"No," said Lady Procula. She was still shaking, but her voice was under control. "I don't want any of that. Leave me, all of you – except Julia."

Julia plumped the pillows around her as the other staff hurried silently away. "I think you should have the drink, madam," she said. "You'll feel better for it."

"I know what you're trying to do," said Lady Procula. "You're offering all the things that would help me go back to sleep, but I don't want to sleep."

"As you wish, madam," said Julia. If the dream had been so terrible, Lady Procula might be afraid to go back to sleep. "Do you want to tell me what the nightmare was?"

"Oh, it wasn't really a nightmare," said Lady Procula. She was calmer now, sitting up against the pillows. "At the end, yes, it was terrible. But I dreamed I saw Jesus of Nazareth and he was such a *good* man."

Julia nearly asked, "How did you know it was him?" but stopped herself in time. It was a dream, and people know things in dreams.

"What was he doing?" she asked.

Lady Procula frowned. Dreams are strange things to explain, like trying to catch a bird in flight.

"I don't think he was doing anything," she said. "It was the way I felt. Everything about him was right, as if I could see all the way through him and he was good all the way through. Most people aren't like that, even the best of us, but he gave me a feeling of deep wellbeing. I felt… I felt as if he lifted a black stone out of my heart and put in a diamond."

Julia waited. She still didn't know why Lady Procula had screamed.

"Then the darkness was there," said Lady Procula, hugging a pillow. "Somebody was burning something and the smoke billowed up as if it would suffocate us both. Then something was crushing us – and a voice shouted…"

Her hands curled. Her voice dropped as she said the word.

"Crucify."

Julia tried to think of something helpful to say. There wasn't anything. The word was going round that Rabbi Jesus of Nazareth was to be tried today. He'd appear before Pilate, Lady Procula's husband, and he probably would be crucified. As far as Julia could see, he hadn't done anything to deserve it.

Crucifixion was for murderers and the most dangerous criminals. Healing sick people and telling stories – what was the matter with that?

"The voice said 'crucify'," repeated Lady Procula. "And it was my husband's voice."

She wriggled out of bed and pushed her feet into her sandals. "Help me dress, Julia. I need to get to my husband. He needs to know Jesus is innocent."

"Madam," Julia warned her, "it's not safe for you to go running across the city. And it's not good for your dignity either. Let me go."

"No, not you!" said Lady Procula. "If I'm staying, you're staying. Can we send one of the servants?"

"Marcus is a good runner, madam," said Julia. "We can send him in the morning, first thing, before the trial begins."

"He must tell Pilate this from me," ordered Lady Procula. "Have nothing to do with that innocent man. I have suffered much because of a dream about him."

Before dawn Julia gave the message to Marcus and sent him running to Pilate. All day she struggled to keep Lady Procula occupied with household business – menus, new fabrics for the couches, and the choice of a new mosaic for the bathroom – until Pilate returned.

When Pilate came home at last, Lady Procula ran to meet him. Before she could ask, he was answering her question.

"Don't worry," he said, reaching out his hands to her. "I got your message."

"So you didn't have him crucified?" she demanded.

"I didn't," he said. "I felt just as you did. I didn't want anything to do with it. I passed him back to his own people. I washed my hands and let them get on with it. It was their decision, not mine."

Lady Procula took a step back.

"What do you mean?"

"I mean it was up to them. They wanted him crucified."

Her hands flew to her face. Julia, watching, saw her grow pale again.

"You let it happen!" whispered Lady Procula.

"Yes," he said and shrugged, annoyed at her for not understanding. "You're the one who said I should have nothing to do with him."

Lady Procula ran to her room and stayed there, letting nobody but Julia come near her.

All night and all the next day she sobbed, crying out that this was not meant to happen; it wasn't what she meant – Pilate should have protected him. Finally Julia persuaded her to take a soothing drink and she slept.

It was Sunday morning when she woke. Again, her hair was tangled and her eyes were small and pink from crying, but she was calm. She almost smiled at Julia as she sat up.

"I had another dream," she said.

Mary of Magdala

IF YOU ASKED Mary who was the most important person in her life, she'd say, "Jesus." If you asked, "Who was the most important person in your life before Jesus?" she'd have to think about it. Then she'd say, "There wasn't anyone."

Life hadn't been good to Mary. Family had let her down. Men had treated her badly and friends had never stayed for long. For a woman alone, money was hard to come by, so Mary of Magdala managed as best she could. It was a lonely life and not a good one. And Mary thought, "I must be a bad person. Not even my family want me. I can't keep friends. I must be wicked."

She knew people thought badly of her. Friends from childhood, who were now married with children of their own, would avoid her eyes. They gathered into close, chattering groups to make sure she stayed an outsider. She would have liked to help old people with their shopping and be an adopted aunt to other people's children, but how could she do that when everyone avoided her?

"Then it's your loss, not mine," she thought bitterly and held her head high. She still had her pride.

So who were they gossiping about today? For once, it wasn't Mary. They were talking about Jesus of Nazareth, Jesus the healer, the teacher. They were saying he had the power to cast out evil spirits and heal the sick. They said he

spoke out for the poor, teaching that God was on their side.

"So why are they still poor?" thought Mary.

Apparently Jesus said that anyone could be his friend. Everybody was welcome to the kingdom of God. "Not me," thought Mary.

On one very bad day, when people had called her terrible names in the street, when there was no bread in the house and no money to buy any, and Mary was in a bad temper, she decided to go and meet Jesus. "Goody-goody Jesus," she thought. "I'll make a scene. See what he makes of that!"

Jesus was sitting in the house of a friend with a crowd around him. He glanced up, smiled and nodded as if he knew her, said, "Hello, Mary," and went on talking.

Mary was too astonished to speak. How did he know her name? People must have been talking about her. *That bad woman.* Then Jesus moved over and made space for her on the seat beside him, but she didn't choose to sit there, not that day.

But the next day she went back and did sit beside him. And the next. He talked and she listened. Then she talked and he listened until all the poison of envy, bitterness, resentment, hatred, misery, pride, and dishonesty flew from her, because there was no room for them in her life any more. She felt clean, as if she had washed in pure, sparkling water.

And then came the day when darkness seemed to seep right into her. She watched Jesus die so horribly that she prayed for his last breath to come soon.

Now that his body has lain cold in the tomb all the sabbath day, she will go to him to wash his body clean, as if she were family. It is the last thing she can do for him. She is ready before dawn for her walk to this place of the dead, carrying towels and spices and an empty bowl, which she fills with water from the spring on the hillside. In her purse she has the little money she owns, because she may have to pay someone to open the tomb for her. It is a job for strong arms. Her eyes hurt, because she has wept for two days and two sleepless nights.

When she sees that the tomb is already open, she thinks that the first early morning light is playing tricks on her sore eyes and aching mind – but there is no mistake. The tomb where they laid his wrapped body is open – and empty. He is not there. There isn't even a body to grieve over. She has nothing.

Her legs tremble and she has to kneel so she doesn't fall. Her head is spinning.

A man is speaking to her and she tries to pull herself together. In the bowl of water she can see her own face, red-eyed and haggard. She supposes that the man must be the gardener and asks him where the body of Jesus has been placed.

"Mary," he says.

Mary.

Nobody else says her name like that. She splashes water on to her face, dabs her eyes on the towel until they are clear, and looks up.

She sees him. And the water in the bowl sparkles like sunlight on the sea.

Lydia

IN THYATIRA, WE all went around with purple hands and smelled like rotting fish. That's because we made the world-famous purple dye out of shellfish. Shellfish, yes. Sea snails. It takes twelve thousand snails to produce enough dye for a little bit of purple cloth – just about enough to make a blanket for an emperor's baby – so our dye is *very* exclusive. Only emperors and the absolute top people are allowed to wear it, which is just as well, because nobody else can afford it.

There was money in the cloth trade and I did well. By the time I moved to Philippi, I wasn't making the dye myself any more – I was selling the best purple cloth in the Roman empire. I had good people working for me, too, both in the cloth business and in my household. I think it's shameful to earn a lot of money and keep it to yourself, so I paid my staff well and looked after them, and they looked after me. I had an excellent trade and a good team.

I don't take all the credit for myself – no. I believe that when God gives you a gift, he wants to see you make the most of it. God gave me the gift of being a good businesswoman and I always remembered to thank him for it.

When you work with dye, you get to look at colour very precisely. You notice every change in a shade and every variation in a pattern, and do you know

what that taught me? God loves colour. Come sunrise and sunset, he throws out astonishing reds and golds. By day exquisite blues drift and blend in the sky. Have you seen how many greens there are in a field of grass? I think in colours. Peace is pale blue and calm is soft green like reeds and lilypads on quiet water. Bright yellow is joy and reds can be anything from love to joy to death.

Take purple, for example. Purple is beautiful, but because the emperors wear it, everyone in the Roman empire sees it as power and money. *Proud purple.* Sea snails by the million, years of experience, and hours of work to make one bolt of purple cloth, but look at the work of God. He's extravagant with purple. He grows purple crocuses and figs, sage, geraniums, bilberries. He flings colour about.

There was a little group of us who used to meet once a week to pray, and whenever we could, we prayed at a place by the river, with God's blue sky above us and his beautiful world all around. On one particular sabbath day, we had company.

Four men came to join us and what a mixed bunch they were! There was Paul, who came from Tarsus, a short man going bald. He was the leader, the one who did most of the talking, and he and his friend Silas had been working together for a long time.

The others – nice Dr Luke and young Timothy – seemed to have stuck to Paul like burrs on his travels.

They joined us for prayer and then asked us if we'd heard of Jesus of Nazareth. We hadn't, so Dr Luke started to tell Jesus' story, and as he talked, it came to life in my head. I could imagine Jesus teaching on green hillsides and walking the dry, dusty roads. I could see his trial and execution, his rough cross, the blood, and the purple robe he wore (oh, how I hoped it wasn't one of mine). And when he talked about Jesus rising from the tomb, I could see the pale gold sky and fresh greens of the perfect morning. That very day I was baptized as a follower of Jesus. So were the household staff. And the workforce. It just seemed the right thing to do.

I invited all four of our visitors home afterwards. They didn't have a clue where they were going to eat or sleep, so I gathered them up and took them in. They hesitated, because Paul couldn't wait to go off and preach somewhere and Dr Luke said he didn't want to put me to any trouble, but I wasn't taking no for an answer. Then one of them pointed out that Jesus told his followers to stay where they were welcome, so that decided it. They all came to stay.

Then, suddenly, we were all at the centre of a local scandal! There were two men working in Philippi and there was definitely something shady about them.

Creepy. They were showmen of some sort and they'd got this poor disturbed young servant girl with them. She told fortunes and they made a lot of money out of her. The strange thing was that she could tell that there was something special about Paul and Silas, because she followed them around, shouting that they were the servants of the one true God and everyone should listen to them.

That sounds like a good thing, but it really wasn't. In the first place, Paul could tell that the poor girl was being controlled by an evil spirit, and secondly, she was driving him around the bend. Finally he turned to face her and in the name of Jesus, he cast the bad spirit out of her.

She calmed down completely after that. She stopped following them around. She stopped the fortune telling, too, so those two showmen were furious. They'd done very well out of that girl and wanted to get their own back, so this is what they did. They dragged Paul and Silas before the council and told a lot of lies about them, and there was very nearly a riot. Paul and Silas were blamed, beaten black and blue, and thrown into prison. And they were Roman citizens, too! Nobody was allowed to treat Roman citizens like that!

"What can we do?" I asked Dr Luke.

"Do what Paul and Silas are doing in prison," he said. "Pray."

So pray we did and trusted God to act. We hadn't expected an earthquake in the middle of the night! Our house shook a little, as if somebody had banged a door, but the prison was right in the centre of the quake. The doors of Paul and Silas's cell flew open. Paul and Silas could have got away, but they didn't. They stayed to look after the jailer.

The poor jailer was panicking, because he thought he'd lost his prisoners, and he could be put to death for that. He'd drawn his sword to kill himself, poor soul – I suppose he wanted to get it over quickly – but Paul and Silas stayed put and calmed him down. They talked to him about Jesus. He ended up taking them to his own house for a wash and a good meal, and by the morning, he'd been baptized. He and all his family!

Also, by morning, the fuss had died down and the jailer was ordered to let Paul and Silas go free. Paul couldn't resist it. He pointed out that he and Silas were Roman citizens, and the council had trampled on their rights.

I gather the council were thoroughly shaken, and no wonder! You can get into awful trouble for breaking Roman law like that. They asked Paul and Silas, very politely, if they would kindly leave the city. Immediately, please. And quietly.

"Certainly not!" said Paul and Silas. "We want you to give us a safe escort out of the city. Things might get violent again."

They insisted on coming back to my house first, to collect their things and say goodbye to us all. Paul was keen to go on taking the gospel to new places, so he wasn't too worried about being thrown out of Philippi. That sort of thing happened to him a lot.

We keep in touch with them. I've got some good woollen fabrics in now, so I'll make cloaks for them all. Paul's always moving on in a hurry and forgetting his cloak. How can you forget a thing like that? We sent him a parcel a little while ago, and what a lovely letter he sent back! Such a warm, encouraging letter. I've kept it. We still read it, over and over again.